OBEDIENCE

by Jane Buerger
illustrated by Helen Endres

THE CHILD'S WORLD

Mankato, MN 56001

Library of Congress Cataloging in Publication Data

Buerger, Jane.
  Obedience.

  (What is it?)
  SUMMARY: Presents situations that exemplify the
nature of obedience.
  1. Obedience—Juvenile literature. (1. Obedience)
I. Endres, Helen. II. Title
BJ1459.B83 1981   179'.9   80-39520
ISBN 0-89565-206-4

What is obedience?

Obedience is following rules that are made to protect and help us.

When Mom or Dad says, "No" to a
TV program, obeying is turning off the
set cheerfully.

When you go to the amusement park
with a friend, and your parents tell you,
''Do not go on the roller coaster,''
obeying is not going—even though Mom
and Dad would never know.

When Dad says Chips is not to stay in the house at night, obeying is not slipping him inside.

When Mom says, "Drink your milk,"
and she's called to the phone, obeying is
not feeding the milk to Tabby.

14

When you're on a vacation trip and your parents ask you to ride quietly for awhile, obeying is looking at a picture book or coloring a picture.

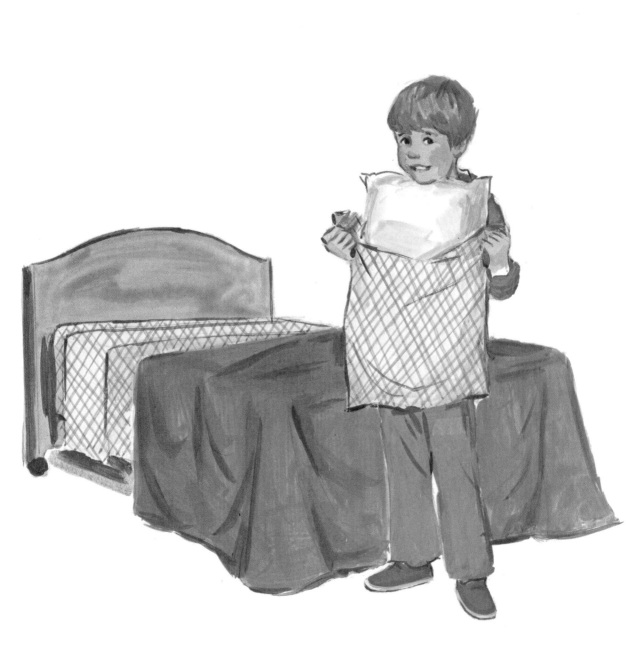

Making your bed,

and hanging up your clothes, just as
Mother asked you to do, that's obeying.

When the teacher says, "Line up
behind each other to go home," obeying
is not running to the front but going
to the end of the line.

When you're at a red light, and you see
your best friend across the street, and
he's hurrying away, obeying is waiting
for the light to turn green.

When your parents leave you with a babysitter and tell you to go to bed at eight o'clock, obeying is not begging to stay up later.

Obeying is staying inside as Mother
asked you to do, when everyone else is
outside building a snowman.

Obeying is following your teacher's rules when she's sick and you have a substitute.

When you see a sign on the grass that reads, "Keep off," and you could sneak across to get your ball, but you walk around instead, that's obeying.

KEEP OFF!

When you wait for the crossing guard
to tell you to cross, that's obedience.

Can you think of other ways to be
obedient?